Drop Zone

Mike Gould

Folens

United Kingdom: Folens Publishers, Apex Business Centre, Boscombe Road, Dunstable, LU5 4RL.
Email: folens@folens.com

Ireland: Folens Publishers, Greenhills Road, Tallaght, Dublin 24.
Email: info@folens.ie

Poland: JUKA, ul. Renesansowa 38, Warsaw 01-905.

Editor: Kay Macmullan
Layout artist: Lee Williams
Cover design: Duncan McTeer
Illustrations: Josephine Blake

First published 2003 by Folens Limited.

British Library Cataloguing in Publication Data. A catalogue record for this publication is available from the British Library.

ISBN 1 84303 388–7

Contents

The story so far

If you haven't read an *On the edge* book before:
The stories take place in and around a row of shops and buildings called Pier Parade in Brightsea, right next to the sea. There's Big Fry, the fish and chip shop; Drop Zone, the drop-in centre for local teenagers; Macmillan's, the sweet and souvenir shop; Anglers' Haven, the fishing tackle shop; the Surf 'n' Skate shop and, of course, the Brightsea Beach Bar.

If you have read an *On the edge* book you may have met some of these people before.

Nathan Brown:	*a bit of a loner, Nathan's great love is snooker.*
June Longley:	*runs Drop Zone, the drop-in centre for local teenagers. Always busy, June is friendly and a good listener.*
Joolz Baker:	*a frequent visitor at Drop Zone, Joolz has a talent for sport.*

So, what's been going on?
Drop Zone survived the storm – just about – and the manager, June, has got the place up and running again. It still remains the best place for people to hang out, or escape their worries, and that's what draws Joolz and Nathan to it.

What happens in this story?
Nathan's a future snooker star. Unfortunately, he picks the wrong opponents in Dan and Matt. Matt's out to get him, and sees the perfect chance for revenge at the Drop Zone snooker tournament.

1

Right on cue

Nathan lined up the shot into the far corner.

The other three balls were in impossible positions.

If he got this shot, he would win.

The older boy watched him.
His friend in the blue sweatshirt watched too.

"That's easy, that is ..." Blue Sweatshirt said.
He moved closer to the snooker table.
Nathan looked up.

It wasn't fair.
They were trying to put him off.

Nathan calmed himself.

He took a deep breath, then smoothly stroked the white ball.

It clattered against the brown ball.
It shot down the table.
It looked as though it would go straight into the hole.

But, at the last moment, Blue Sweatshirt leant against the table.

The ball wobbled.
It bounced into the jaws of the pocket.

It should have dropped.
But it didn't.

It rolled, and then popped out.

Nathan couldn't believe it.
"You made that happen!" he said.

Blue Sweatshirt smiled.
"Me? What did I do?"

"My shot," said the older boy.

He took his cue.

The shot was easy now.
The brown was right over the pocket.

He knocked it in.

"That's £5 you owe me," he said to Nathan.

Nathan looked at him.
Blue Sweatshirt moved over to stand next to his mate.

"Come on then. Give us it."

"I haven't got it," Nathan said.

“What?”

“I … I thought …”

“What did you think?” said
Blue Sweatshirt.

“Nothing,” said Nathan. “I can get it
though. Soon,” he added.

Blue Sweatshirt laughed.
It was a nasty laugh.

“Soon isn’t any good. I think we need to
teach you a lesson now.”

The older boy and Blue Sweatshirt moved
towards Nathan.
They were on the other side of the table.

Nathan saw his chance.
He grabbed his cue and the case, and
started to run.

"Oi!" shouted the man who ran the snooker club.

Blue Sweatshirt and the older boy brushed past the man.

They chased after Nathan.

But he was already outside the snooker club.

The beach and Pier Parade were only two hundred metres away.

He could lose them there.

2

Lock up

June locked the door of Drop Zone.
It was 10 pm.

The centre was supposed to shut at 9.30.
But June, who ran Drop Zone, didn't have the heart to throw some of the kids out.

She knew they didn't want to go home.
She really liked the kids.

Though they hated being called that,
'The kids'.
"Don't call us that, June," they said.
"It sucks!"

So, June always tried to learn their names.
But it wasn't easy.

The Drop Zone was supposed to be for young people who didn't have anything to do.
Boys and girls came there to get away from their parents.
Or to get away from troubles at school.
Basically, they just 'dropped in'.

They liked the Zone even though there was quite a lot to do in the town.
There were plenty of nightclubs.
And there was the sports centre.
But nothing was cheap.

Sometimes all they wanted to do was hang about and chat.
Send each other messages on their mobiles.

June thought, 'If I had a fiver for every time I'd heard someone say "Text us, yeh?" I'd be rich by now!'

She started to walk along the parade.

As usual, there was a small group still sitting on the steps that led up to the road.

Some were smoking.
Two were kissing each other.
Those two didn't notice June!
But the others called out.
"See ya, June!"

She turned around.
Then she smiled and waved.

"Bye!" she said.

As she went to turn back, a figure almost knocked her over.

It was a boy.
He had his hood up, and was carrying a long, thin case.
Who was it?

Before she had a chance to speak, he had run past her on to the parade.

Soon he was out of sight.

June sighed and carried on walking up the steps.

At the top she was almost knocked over again!

This time it was two boys.
The older boy was panting.
He leant on his long case.

It was like the one the first boy was carrying.

The one in the blue sweatshirt leant over the railing.

"We've lost him because of you," he said. "You need to lose some weight if I'm gonna be your manager. Snooker players aren't fat no more."

"Sorry," gasped the other one.

June watched as the two boys turned and started to walk away.

3

Club night

June recognised him the moment he came into Drop Zone.

He was carrying the case again.
As if it was his pride and joy.

His hood was up so she couldn't see his face.
But it was him all right.

June didn't speak to him.
She'd wait until he spoke to her.

He seemed to know a few people there, but he hadn't come to chat.

He went straight over to the snooker table.

It was an old, battered one the snooker club had given to the centre.

No one used it much.

Snooker wasn't very fashionable.

Anyway, half the balls were missing. And there was a rip in the baize.

But, to Nathan, it was better than nothing. He set up the balls in position and started practising.

He was good.
Very good.

Soon, a small crowd gathered around.

"Look at that trick shot he just did," said one girl.

"That was brilliant," said her brother. "I can't even hit the ball!"

Nathan showed off a bit.

Eventually another boy came forward and asked him for a game.

It didn't take long.

Whack! Plop!
Smack! Plop!

Each ball dropped into the hole.

Only once or twice did Nathan miss. That was when the torn baize caught his ball.

At 9.30 June called out, "We're closing. Bring your drinks and any rubbish over to the kitchen."

People began to drift away.

Nathan was still on the snooker table. Practising.

Soon he was the only one left.

June spoke to him.
"We're closing now."

He looked up.
He still had his hood on.

"Come back tomorrow. We open at the same time."

"Thanks," said Nathan.

He popped his cue into the snooker case and disappeared.

4

Nathan makes a friend

Nathan came the next night.
And the next club night after that.

He spent the whole time practising.

Some nights he had to take his turn.
Other kids decided it would be cool
to play.

One even asked Nathan to show him the
best shots.

Nathan was patient.
"Keep your head down low over the cue.
Stay still."

It was a girl.
Julie.
Or Joolz, as the others called her.

She was good.
A real natural.

Nathan showed her lots of new shots.
She picked them up quickly.

Then some others wanted to play, so Nathan and Joolz went over to the kitchen.

Joolz got them a can of Coke each.

"Have you played before?" asked Nathan.

"Yeah," said Joolz. "A bit. My dad used to have a half-size table in the garage. But he got rid of it."

"You're good," said Nathan.

"Not as good as you. You could be on the telly."

Nathan sighed.
"No I couldn't. I need good tables. Lots of competition."

Joolz put her cup down.
"What about the snooker club?"
she asked.

"Nah. Can't go there anymore."

"Why not?"

"Just can't."

Joolz could see Nathan didn't want to talk about it.

Then she had an idea.
"We can't do much about the table,
but we could have a competition."

5

Window looking

Blue Sweatshirt and the other boy, whose name was Dan, stood outside the shop window.

"Look. A competition. At that stupid Drop Zone place," said Blue Sweatshirt. "You'll win that, dead easy."

Dan wasn't so sure.
"There could be some good players there."

"Hello?" said Blue Sweatshirt, grabbing Dan by the shoulders. "A place like that? Give me a break! It'll be full of losers."

"There's no prize," said Dan.

"No – but we can make some bets with the kids there. You can pretend to be really crap. That shouldn't be difficult!"

Blue Sweatshirt laughed at his own joke.

"Shut up, Matt!" said Dan.

Sometimes Matt (Blue Sweatshirt) really got on his nerves.

All this stuff about being his manager.
It was stupid.

Dan knew he wasn't that good.
He liked playing, but that was about it.

"Right. Let's go up the snooker club," said Matt.

"What? I'm starving. My tea'll be ready soon."

"Stop thinking about your stomach. Like I said, you need to lose weight. And you need to practise."

Matt started walking towards the snooker club.
"Come on! Or do you want to go to Fat Club instead?!"

Dan sighed.

He stuck his hand into his trouser pocket. There was half a Mars bar in there.

He stuffed it into his mouth in one go.

So what if Matt saw?
Dan didn't care.

6

Match play

Drop Zone was full.

June was pleased.
She liked to see it used by lots of kids.

There were quite a few she hadn't seen before.

The snooker table had been polished.
Nathan had managed to mend the tear in the baize with some special glue.

It looked quite good.
Almost decent.

It was near the end of the tournament, which had lasted most of the afternoon.

It was now eight o'clock.
There were even a few mums and dads hanging around.

But they had stayed outside.
Or gone to the 3Bs for a coffee.
Their children didn't want them watching over them.

The semi-final had begun.

Nathan was playing another boy from the centre.
He was quite good, but Nathan was winning.
He already had forty points on the board.
The boy only had three.

Soon, Nathan had only the pink to pot in order to win.

In it went!

He was in the final.

He shook hands with the boy.

“Bad luck!” he said.

He went to get a drink.
Joolz was by the kitchen.

He wanted to talk to her anyway.
“Hi,” he said.

“Hi,” she replied in a shaky voice.

“What’s the matter?” he asked.

“I’m nervous, that’s what! I never thought I’d make the semi-final.”

“You deserve it!” said Nathan.

They looked over towards the table.

Nathan pointed at the boy who was practising.
“See him?”

"The one I'm playing?"

"Yeah."

"What about him?" asked Joolz.

"He's the reason I stopped going to the snooker club. Well, him and his mate."

"What? The one in the blue sweatshirt?"

"He always wears that sweatshirt," said Nathan. "His name's Matt."

Nathan took a big swig from his Coke can.

"He cheated me out of a game. He jogged the table as I was about to win. Says I owe him £5. First thing Blue Sweatshirt did when he arrived was to remind me. Said I'd better pay up. Or else he and his mate would beat me up."

"Have you got the money?" asked Joolz.

"No. But I will have."

"When?"

"After your game. I bet him £50 you'd beat him."

"What?" said Joolz.
She looked stunned.
"What if I lose?"

"You're not gonna lose."

Joolz started to walk away.

Half-way towards the table she turned and pointed a finger at him.

"You're mad. Don't expect me to save you when I get beaten!"

7

Battle on the baize

Everybody in the centre was crowded round for the match.

Some stood on chairs.
Some stood on the old tables.

Joolz nervously polished her cue.

Matt took Dan to one side.

"You've got it in the bag, mate. It's only a girl. You'll walk it. Like I said."

Dan wasn't so sure.
"She looked good in the last round."

"Nah. Her opponent was crap. She was lucky. Once you get your fat backside in front, she'll give up."

Dan gritted his teeth.
He took a step towards Matt.

"Don't call me fat! All right?"

"Calm down. I was only joking."

"That's what you always say," said Dan. "Anyway, why are you so keen for me to win? What are you gonna get out of it?"

"Never you mind," said Matt, half-grinning.

Dan stepped forward and picked up his cue.
Joolz had lost the toss.

Matt moved round to where Nathan was watching.

"Don't forget, snooker boy. Fifty quid."

8

Key moment

The game had lasted forty minutes.

It was desperately close.
Joolz had been in the lead for most of the time.

But she had just missed an easy shot.

Dan looked at the table.

He could go for red in the middle pocket.
Or he could play safe.

That would be the clever shot.

Aim to get the white ball somewhere Joolz couldn't escape from.

He bent down ready to play his shot.

Just then Matt leant forward.

"Go for it, mate. Drop that red ball."

Dan stopped just in time.

"I can't. It's too difficult."

"No it's not," Matt whispered. "You get that, and we're twenty quid better off."

"What?"

"Twenty quid. I bet Snooker Boy twenty quid you'd beat her."

Dan swore under his breath.

How dare Matt make the bet!
He wasn't the one playing.

Dan started to sweat.
What if he missed?
He didn't have twenty quid.

He aimed the ball for the middle pocket.

He tried to steady himself.
His hands were so sweaty he could hardly hold the cue.

He played the shot.

It missed!

Even worse, he'd left the red ball over the corner pocket.

Joolz stepped up and put it in.

Easy!

She felt confident.
All the remaining balls were in good positions.

Bang! Down went the black.

Bang! Down went the yellow.

She looked at the scoreboard.

All she needed was the green.
Then she'd win.

She was in a perfect position.

She leant forward, pulled back the cue.
Gently she rolled the white ball towards the green.

It made a perfect contact.

Slowly and surely it rolled towards the pocket.

Then, out of the corner of her eye, she saw Matt lean forward.

He was going to jog the table!
Just as he had at the snooker club!

Everyone was watching the ball.
No one would see!

No one, that is, except Dan.

"No!" Dan said, pushing Matt back.
Matt struggled, but Dan was too strong.

The ball dropped into the pocket!

Everyone cheered!

June stepped forward.
"Joolz wins!"

Matt was red-faced and angry.
Dan still had him by the sweatshirt.

"What d'you do that for, you prat?"
said Matt.

"She beat me fair and square,"
replied Dan.

"You realise what that's cost us?
Fifty quid!"

Dan let Matt go.

"Fifty quid? You said twenty!"

Matt looked even redder.
He hadn't meant to tell Dan.

"So you were going to pocket the rest for yourself?" Dan said.

"I was gonna tell you. Honest." said Matt.

"Yeh. Right," said Dan. "I'm sick of your comments about me. And sick of snooker. It's a joke, you managing me."

Nathan appeared on one side, with Joolz next to him.

"I think you owe us some money,"
he said.

Dan pushed Matt away from him.

"Wrong," he said. "My manager does. Or should I say, my *ex-manager.*"

9

Final thoughts

Joolz and Nathan made their way back towards the table.
But June blocked their path.

"Sorry, guys. It's all over for tonight."

"What?" said Nathan.

"What about the final?" added Joolz.

"You'll have to play next week. Have you seen the time? I'll have parents bashing down the door if I don't let you all go."

June walked towards the kitchen.

Most of the others had got the message and were already leaving.

Joolz and Nathan weren't in a hurry.

But June had lots of clearing up to do.

It would have to wait.

"So it's you and me next week, then?" said Nathan.

"Looks like it. But I could do with some extra practice. Otherwise you'll destroy me," said Joolz. "Won't be much fun. For you or me."

"No problem," said Nathan. "I know just the place."

"Where?" said Joolz.

"The snooker club. I'm already a member."

"But I'm not. Doesn't it cost loads to join?"

Nathan smiled and picked up his cue. He slipped it into the case.

"Yeah."

He snapped the lid down.

"I seem to remember it was about £50."